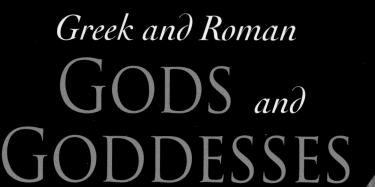

Greek and Roman

GODS and GODDESSES

by Brendan Walsh

Table of Contents

INTRODUCTION

In the ancient world, the Greeks and Romans worshipped many gods. There was a god or goddess for almost everything. There were too many to count. There was a god or goddess for every river, every mountain, every town, every village, and every part of daily life.

Some gods were more important than others. The twelve most important gods were called the Olympians. The Olympians were mostly the same in Greek **mythology** and Roman mythology. The Romans conquered Greece in 146 B.C.E. They copied the Greek gods and made them their own. This is why most of the gods have two names—a Greek name and a Roman name.

The Temple of Zeus is in Athens, Greece. It is 2,500 years old.

ZEUS

Of all the gods, none was more powerful than Zeus, "King of the Gods." He was the leader of the twelve Olympians. Most of them lived on the top of a mountain called Mount Olympus.

Zeus was the youngest son of Cronus and Rhea. Cronus and Rhea belonged to an older group of gods called the Titans. Cronus was the king of the Titans. He was afraid that his children would overthrow his rule, so he imprisoned them.

Cronus's wife Rhea hid Zeus away on the island of Crete. When Zeus grew up, he freed his siblings and overthrew his Titan father. Zeus and his brothers divided Earth among them. Zeus claimed the sky as his.

The ancient Greeks believed Zeus controlled the weather. He was known as "The Cloud Gatherer." Zeus could throw lightning bolts from his hand. He used lightning and thunder as weapons against his enemies. The Greeks believed that the wind came from Zeus's **aegis**. An aegis is a shield attached to a cape.

The Greeks believed Zeus was fair, but he was not friendly. Zeus was easily angered. He became furious when he was lied to or when promises were broken. Even other powerful gods were afraid of Zeus's temper.

When in Rome...

The Roman name for Zeus was Jupiter, or Jove. Like Zeus, Jupiter was "King of the Gods." Romans referred to Jupiter as "The Light Bringer."

OLYMPIC ORIGINS

The ancient Greeks held a festival in honor of Zeus every four years—the Olympics. Like the modern-day Olympics, the festival was centered on sports and games. All the major cities in Greece sent their best athletes to compete.

HERA

The mighty Zeus feared no man, but he did fear one woman, his wife Hera. Hera was the goddess of women, marriage, and childbirth. She was "Queen of the Gods." She was the most important goddess in ancient Greece. Some of the earliest and largest temples the Greeks ever built were made for Hera.

Hera and Zeus had four children together. Each of them became gods and goddesses. But Zeus also had children with other women. This made Hera very jealous.

When in Rome...

The Roman name for Hera was Juno. She was also the queen of the gods and a goddess of marriage. The month of June is named after her. Romans believed June was the best month for marriage. Unlike Hera, Juno was also a goddess of war. Juno could wield lightning bolts like her husband.

Because she was filled with jealousy, Hera spent much of her time plotting revenge. She did not like the children that Zeus had with other women. Heracles, for example, was the son of Zeus and a woman named Alcmene. Hera tried to destroy Heracles throughout his life. She even put snakes in his cradle. The Roman name for Heracles was Hercules.

Peacocks were sacred' to Hera. Peacock feathers have a shape that looks like an eye. The "eyes" symbolized that Hera watched over everything. Peacocks grazed freely in the temples the Greeks built for Hera.

HERACLES THE HERO

Heroes in ancient Greece and Rome were often part human and part god. They had special powers like the gods, but they were not immortal. That meant they could die.

7

POSEIDON

Master of the sea, protector of cities, Poseidon was feared and respected throughout the ancient world. Poseidon was one of Zeus's brothers. Poseidon helped Zeus overthrow the rule of the Titans. As a reward, he became the god of the sea.

Poseidon carried a weapon called a **trident**. A trident is a spear with three points. Sometimes Poseidon struck the ground with his trident. The ancient Greeks believed this caused earthquakes. They also thought it caused shipwrecks. For this reason, Poseidon was also known as "The Earth Shaker."

Poseidon was also a god of horses. He rode on a **chariot** when he traveled. Magical horses called hippocamps pulled Poseidon's chariot. Hippocamps were half horse and half fish. They ran on top of the water.

The ancient Greeks built many temples to honor Poseidon. This was very important for cities on the coast. These cities often named Poseidon as their patron, or protector. Sailors made sacrifices to Poseidon before voyages. They hoped this would please Poseidon. But Poseidon did not feel pleased often. Like the sea, Poseidon was dangerous and unpredictable.

R*When in* *ome...*

Neptune was the Roman name for Poseidon. Unlike Poseidon, Neptune was a god of freshwater as well as the sea. He was important to people who counted on rivers and lakes for crops.

ATHENA

Brave, bold, clever, and courageous, the goddess Athena was a force to be reckoned with. Athena was a daughter of Zeus. She did not have a mother. She was born straight out of Zeus's forehead. The Greeks thought that Athena was Zeus's favorite daughter.

Athena was the goddess of wisdom, mathematics, strength, and courage. She was also a goddess of war. She was strong and she wore powerful armor. But she was not like the god of war, Ares. Ares enjoyed war and fighting, but Athena did not. She preferred to use wisdom to sort out problems and avoid war.

The Greek city-state of Athens was named after Athena. According to myth, there was a contest between Athena and Poseidon. The winner became the patron of the city. Poseidon and Athena each gave one gift to the people of the city. The citizens judged the gifts. It was up to them to choose which god they wanted as their protector.

Athena's gift was to create the world's first olive tree. Athena's olive tree gave them food, shade, and oil. Poseidon used his trident to make a magical spring of flowing water. The spring that Poseidon made was too salty and the citizens could not drink it. They chose Athena and named the city Athens.

R*When in* *Rome...*

Minerva was the Roman name for Athena. Like Athena, Minerva was also the goddess of war and wisdom. Minerva was more connected to artists, craftsmen, and thinkers. She was often shown with an owl as a symbol of her wisdom.

11

Fierce and full of rage, Ares caused even the strongest walls to crumble. He was the Greek god of war and holder of awesome power. He was the first-born son of Zeus and Hera. He was not liked among the gods. He was hateful, violent, and cruel. The ancient Greeks did not trust Ares and they believed that Ares never wanted war to end.

There were very few temples or sculptures built for Ares. The city of Sparta was the exception. Sparta was a city of warriors. They built a statue of Ares bound in chains. This symbolized that war never left the city of Sparta.

When in Rome...

The Romans' name for Ares was Mars. Mars was more than just the god of war. He was also a god of agriculture. Roman warriors worshipped Mars. They thought he could protect them in battle. This was different from the way the Greeks treated the god of war. The Greeks thought he was too destructive to be called upon.

APHRODITE

Aphrodite was the goddess of love and beauty. She was born from a foamy sea near the island of Cyprus. The Greek word *aphros* means "sea foam." Aphrodite was born as an adult, so she had no childhood. Some believed she was the daughter of Zeus. Others thought she belonged to an older group of gods, like the Titans.

Aphrodite was so beautiful that Zeus thought her beauty was dangerous. He worried that all of the other gods would be jealous. For this reason, Zeus married her to the unattractive god Hephaestus.

When in Rome...

The Roman name for Aphrodite was Venus. The Romans thought that Venus was the mother of the Roman people. Venus had a son named Aeneas who fought with the Trojans during the Trojan War. The Trojans lost to the Greeks, and Aeneas ran away to Italy. According to the legend, once Aeneas arrived in Italy, he became the founder of ancient Rome.

Apollo was a god of many talents. Not only was he the god of the sun and the light, but he was also known as a healer. The Greeks called upon him when there was disease. He was usually thought of as a good-natured god and a protector from evil. Apollo did have a dark side. He could cause disease as well as cure it.

Apollo carried a bow and arrow. He was the best archer of all the gods. He was also a musician. Apollo played the **lyre**, an ancient instrument. The Greeks honored Apollo by playing special songs for him. These songs were called **paeans**.

MOTHER OF THE GODS

Artemis and Apollo's mother Leto was a nymph. Nymphs were lesser female gods. They were young and beautiful. They were usually connected to places in nature like a forest, a lake, or a mountain.

Apollo's twin sister Artemis was the goddess of the moon. She loved nothing more than the forest, archery, and hunting. Like her brother, she carried a bow and arrow.

Artemis could talk to animals and tell them what to do. She drove a chariot pulled by golden-horned deer, and traveled with a pack of dogs. Her dogs were so strong that they could even hunt lions. Sometimes Artemis used her dogs or other animals to attack her enemies. In one myth, she had a wild hog attack the god Adonis because he claimed to be a better hunter.

When in Rome...

Apollo was known by the same name and had similar powers in both Greek and Roman mythology. He also had a twin sister in both, but she is known as Diana in Roman mythology. Like Artemis, Diana was also the goddess of the moon and hunting, and she could talk to animals.

HEPHAESTUS

Without Hephaestus, Greek and Roman myths would not be nearly as exciting. He was the creator of almost every magical item in Greek mythology. He was the god of fire and the **forge**.

Hephaestus was the son of Hera. He walked with a limp and was described as ugly. This was very rare for a god. But he was a master craftsman and a blacksmith. Hephaestus built many things for the gods. He built their weapons and armor. He even crafted Zeus's lightning bolts. He also constructed the home of the gods on top of Mount Olympus.

When in Rome...

The Roman name for Hephaestus was Vulcan. Like Hephaestus, Vulcan was the god of fire. The word "volcano" comes from his Roman name.

HADES

Dark, gloomy, and **solitary**, Hades ruled over a world all his own. He was the god of the underworld. He was the older brother of Zeus and Poseidon. Hades did not live on Mount Olympus. He spent most of his time in the underworld.

The ancient Greeks were afraid of Hades. Many would not say his name out loud. But the Greeks did not think that Hades was an evil god. Hades ruled over the dead, but he was not the god of death.

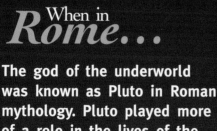

R*ome*... When in

The god of the underworld was known as Pluto in Roman mythology. Pluto played more of a role in the lives of the mortals, while Hades was usually uninterested in the affairs of regular people.

HERMES

The fastest of all the gods was Hermes. His Roman name was Mercury. Hermes was the son of Zeus and the mountain nymph Maia. He was the messenger of the gods. Hermes was known as a friendly and likeable god. The other gods trusted him with their messages. Hermes was one of the youngest gods. He was playful and he liked to play tricks on both humans and gods.

Hermes was the god of boundaries and borders. It was easy for Hermes to travel between the realm of gods and the realm of humans. He was one of only a few gods who knew the way to the underworld. Travelers in ancient Greece prayed to Hermes to keep them safe.

GODLY GEAR

Hermes wore magical winged sandals called talaria. They were made of unbreakable gold. Hephaestus crafted them. They allowed Hermes to fly anywhere and travel very fast.

DEMETER

Demeter was the goddess of the harvest. She had a daughter with Zeus named Persephone. Persephone was the goddess of vegetation. Demeter was best known for her role in the story of Persephone.

Persephone was kidnapped by Hades. Persephone knew if she ate food in the underworld, she would be stuck there forever. So she refused to eat. But after a while, Persephone gave in and ate six pomegranate seeds. Demeter went to Zeus for help, and Zeus made a deal with Hades. Persephone would spend six months of the year in the underworld. For the other six months, Persephone was able to return to the surface. For ancient people, this explained why crops died in the fall and grew again in the spring.

*R*ome... When in

The Roman name for Demeter was Ceres. They were basically the same goddess, but there was a difference with Persephone. The Roman name for Persephone was Proserpine. Proserpine was a goddess of vegetation as well as a goddess of marriage.

CONCLUSION

In modern times, we think of Greek and Roman mythology as stories. However, it's important to remember that people of the ancient world believed it to be real. When lightning struck, it came from the mighty hand of Zeus. An earthquake meant the ill-tempered Poseidon was angry again. A volcanic eruption meant Hephaestus, the blacksmith god, was working at his forge.

The influence of these ancient gods is still felt in modern times. All of the planets in our solar system are named for the Roman gods. Many plants, animals, and chemicals also take the names of the ancient gods. The myths and stories are shared over and over again in new ways in books and film and on television. The gods and goddess of ancient Greece and Rome have lasted the ages.

FAMILY TREE OF THE GODS AND GODDESSES

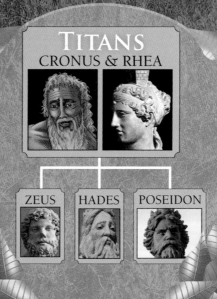

TITANS
CRONUS & RHEA

ZEUS HADES POSEIDON

DEMETER 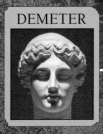 ZEUS 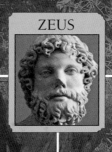 HERA

 APHRODITE  HERMES  ARTEMIS  APOLLO  ATHENA  ARES  HEPHAESTU

GLOSSARY

aegis   (EE-jis) *noun* a shield worn like a cape or a collar as armor (page 5)

chariot   (CHAIR-ee-ut) *noun* a cart that is pulled by horses or other animals (page 9)

forge   (FORJ) *noun* a very hot fireplace used by blacksmiths to heat and shape metal (page 16)

lyre   (LIRE) *noun* a seven-stringed instrument shaped like a harp, but much smaller (page 14)

mythology   (mih-THAH-luh-jee) *noun* a series of stories designed to teach people about the ways of the world (page 3)

paeans   (PEE-unz) *noun* songs, hymns, or poems recited to honor gods (page 14)

solitary   (SAH-lih-tair-ee) *adjective* being or living alone (page 17)

trident   (TRY-dent) *noun* a spear with three points, similar to a pitchfork (page 8)

INDEX

ANALYZE THE TEXT

QUESTIONS FOR CLOSE READING

Use facts and details from the text to support your answers to the following questions.

- From information in this book, how do you know that Greek gods and goddesses showed a lot of emotion?

- The author states that mythology "would not be nearly as exciting" without Hephaestus. Explain why you agree or disagree with this opinion.

- Why was Poseidon particularly important to cities on the coast of ancient Greece?

- On page 3, the author says that Romans copied the Greek gods and made them their own. What details does the author provide to support this claim?

COMPREHENSION: COMPARE AND CONTRAST

Compare and contrast the Greek god Ares to his Roman counterpart Mars. Tell how they are alike and different. Use a Venn diagram to help organize your ideas.

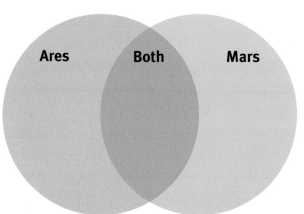

Ares   Both   Mars